COMMENTARY ON THE FC

COMMENTARY ON THE FOURTH GOSPEL

Beryl Pogson

EUREKA EDITIONS

FIRST PUBLISHED PRIVATELY IN 1965

ISBN-10: 90-72395-28-X
ISBN-13: 978-90-72395-28-3

Contents

	Introduction	5
	Foreword	9
I	AUTHORSHIP OF THE FOURTH GOSPEL	11
II	THE LOGOS	14
III	JOHN THE BAPTIST	19
IV	JORDAN	24
V	THE SIX SIGNS	29
VI	THE RAISING OF LAZARUS	37
VII	THE LAST SUPPER	43
VIII	THE HYMN OF JEZUS	49
IX	THE CRUCIFIXION	53
	Appendix	61
	About Beryl Pogson – Photographs	68

COMMENTARY ON THE FOURTH GOSPEL
by
BERYL POGSON (1895-1967)

INTRODUCTION

BERYL POGSON originally printed 100 copies of this book in the 1960s for members of her groups. We were reminded that we were being taught orally and that much is said in the oral teaching that is not found in books; however, she was prompted on many occasions to distil her ideas and formulations into print.

Beryl Pogson was Dr.Maurice Nicoll's pupil for nineteen years and his secretary for fourteen; she worked closely with him helping him with his writings. In her detailed biography of Dr.Nicoll *Maurice Nicoll: A Portrait* (Chapter 10), originally published by Vincent Stuart in 1961 and re-published in 1987 by Fourth Way Books, New York, she describes how these writings developed. Her own understanding of the Gospels she shared with us at meetings and in private talks.

Dr.Nicoll's understanding of the Gospels was published in *The New Man* and *The Mark* and these books have been a source of inspiration and new meaning for many people. Dr.Nicoll said about his intention of writing *The New Man*:

> "The intention is to indicate that all teaching such as contained in the Gospels and many other older and newer teachings, in the short period of known history, is about transcending the violence which characterizes mankind's present level of being. It affirms the possibility of a development of another level of being surmounting violence."

About his teaching Dr.Nicoll said: "Just as we are finding out about all sorts of chemicals, such as the sulphanilamides, penicillin, and streptomycin, so do we have to advance to the study of the poisons of the mind and emotions of which further development were laid down in the Gospels."

It was through reading *The New Man* in 1954, which had been introduced to me by Geoffrey Watkins (Watkins Books Ltd. Cecil Court, London), that I eventually met Beryl Pogson in 1955. I was a member of her group until she died in 1967.

Beryl Pogson spoke to us of the connection with the Greek Mysteries as revealed in the passage in the Fourth Gospel:

> "unless a grain of wheat falls into the earth and dies, it remains alone; but if it dies, it bears much fruit."
>
> (*John* 12:24)

and reminded us that Dr.Nicoll made this very clear in *The Mark* (page 63). She told us that the whole Gospel shows the influence of the Greek Mysteries; and so also on the Passion, if you take Judas as the hierophant who hands over the candidate...

It is certainly time that Beryl Pogson's *Commentary on the Fourth Gospel* is made generally available.

Lewis Creed

Beryl Pogson in 1965

FOREWORD

ACCORDING TO the Johannine tradition referred to by Clement of Alexandria, it was believed that "Christ imparted the truth to James the Just, to John and Peter, after His resurrection". These three disciples were said to share the threefold task of continuing His work – it was said that James the Just, as Bishop of Jerusalem, carried on traditional Christianity, Peter was the organiser and ruled the Church, and John was said to have understood and preserved the spirit of the Teaching. They formed the Triad, which springs from and is closest to the One. There was a similar Triad in the Hermetic tradition in which three disciples of Hermes Trismegistus, Asclepius, Ammon and Tat, represented knowledge, power and love.

G.R.S.Mead quotes from a Codex of the Fourth Gospel, preserved in the Archives of the Templars of St.John of Jerusalem in Paris, certain passages which are additional to the orthodox text:

To John XVII:26

"Amen, I say unto you, I am not of this world, but John shall be your Father, till he shall go with me into Paradise! And He anointed them with the Holy Spirit."

To John XIX:26-30

"He saith to His Mother: 'Weep not, I go to my Father and to Eternal Life – Behold Thy Son, He will keep my place'. Then saith He to the Disciple: 'Behold Thy Mother!' The bowing His Head He breathed forth His Spirit."

Here we find the important statements, "John shall be your Father" and: "He will keep My place."

According the Johannine tradition, the secret spiritual teaching received by John from Christ was handed down orally and survives to this day. Hints of this teaching are found in the Fourth Gospel, the First Epistle of St.John and in a cypher in the Revelation of St.John.

"unless a grain of wheat falls into the earth and dies, it remains alone; but if it dies, it bears much fruit."

(*John* 12:24)

CHAPTER ONE

THE AUTHORSHIP OF THE FOURTH GOSPEL

IN THE Muratorian Canon which contains the first list of New Testament books issued by the Church, compiled in Rome about 170 A.D., the following account of the origin of the Fourth Gospel appears:

> "At the request of his fellow disciples and of his bishops, John, one of the disciples, said: 'Fast with me for three days from this time and whatsoever shall be revealed to each of us, whether it be favourable to my writing or not, let us relate it to one another'. On the same night it was revealed to Andrew that John should relate all things, aided by the remission of all."

Iranaeus, Bishop of Lyons, writes in about 177 A.D.:

> "John, the disciple of the Lord, who also leant upon His breast, himself also published the Gospel in Epheseus, when he was living in Asia."

By the time that the Fourth Gospel was "published" about 100 A.D. (The greek *exedoke* translated "published" means "gave out") John was a hundred years old. He had already written the Book of Revelation during his banishment to the island Patmos, where the Emperor Domitian had sent him, and it is because of what has been called the "barbarous" Greek of this work that scholars have thought that the Gospel and the Letters, which are in excellent Greek, were written down by another hand. A clue to the identity of the writer may be found in a curious statement by Papias, who was Bishop of Hierapolis, near

Ephesus, at that time, who writes that he tried to find out:

> 'what Andrew or what Peter said, or what was said by Philip, by Thomas, or by James, or by John, or by Matthew, or by any other of the disciples of the Lord; and what things Aristion and the Elder John, the disciples of the Lord, say".

Now John the Elder, like St.John, has his tomb in Ephesus, and it is possible that it was he who wrote down in flowing Greek this "spiritual Gospel" as it is later called by Clement of Alexandria. He may have been the Elder referred to in the Second letter:

"The Elder unto the elect lady and her children"

And in the Third Letter:

"The Elder unto the well-beloved Gaius"

Dr.Hugh Schonfield traces a relationship between John, the Beloved Disciple, who was said to have served as a High Priest, and was buried at Ephesus, and John the Elder, a Greek, in the three documents attributed to St.John. He writes in the preface to his translation of the Gospel in the Authentic New Testament:

> "The Gospel contains, in the narrative portions, a great deal that is characteristic of the author of the Revelation, while the Revelation in the Letters to the Seven Churches and some other passages, contains material which is typical of the writer of the Letters and the larger part of the Gospel. The conclusion to which this points is that somehow in the Gospel and the Revelation the works of the Greek Presbyter and the Jewish Priest have been combined. In the Gospel the Greek Presbyter predominates while in the Revelation it is the other way round."

Tradition holds that St.John dictated his Gospel, but Dr.Schonfield thinks that a Dialogue in the Greek Platonic tradition was superimposed on the original Gospel, as in some of the Discourses Jesus speaks as though He were not a Jew and refers to the Law of Moses as "your Law". However, it was the Pharisees from whom Jesus separated Himself, not the Jews as a whole.

It would seem possible that, having taught in Ephesus, a centre of Hellenistic thought, for many years, St.John had expanded his thinking to comprehend the whole background of cosmology which linked Egypt and Greece and Asia Minor, so that he was able to present his Gospel as a universal one, to be understood by Jews and by Gentiles of any race or tradition. One who has had the vision of Patmos could understand the transcendental Being of Christ who was and is to come.

The Letters are written in the Greek of the Elder but the message of the First Letter is the last message of St.John as related by St.Jerome:

> "When John was dying, his disciples asked him if he has any last message to leave them. 'Little children', he said, 'love one another'. Again and again he repeated it; and they asked him if that was all he had to say. 'It is enough,' he said, 'for it is our Lord's command'."

CHAPTER TWO

THE LOGOS

"In the beginning was the word, and the Word was with God, and the Word was God. The same was in the beginning with God. All things were made by him; and without him was not any thing made that was made. In him was life; and the life was the light of men. And the light shineth in darkness; and the darkness comprehended it not. There was a man sent from God, whose name was John. The same came for a witness, to bear witness of the Light, that all men through him might believe. That was the true Light, which lighteth every man that cometh into the world. He was in the world, and the world was made by him, and the world knew him not. He came unto his own, and his own received him not. But as many as received him, to them gave he power to become the sons of God, even to them that believe on his name. Which were born, not of blood, nor of the will of the flesh, nor of the will of man, but of God. And the Word was made flesh, and dwelt among us (and we beheld his glory, the glory as of the only begotten of the Father), full of grace and truth. JOHN bare witness of him, and cried, saying, 'This was he of whom I spake, He that cometh after me is preferred before me: for he was before me. And of his fulness have all we received, and grace for grace. For the law was given by Moses, but grace and truth came by Jesus Christ. No man hath seen God at any time; the only begotten Son, which is in the bosom of the Father, he hath declared him'."

(*John* I, 1-18)

THE ABOVE Prologue to St.John's Gospel is in the form of an antiphonal chant. There is a possibility that it was the Hymn mentioned by Pliny the Younger when he wrote to the Emperor Trajan about the Christians, that "they met on a certain fixed day before it was light and sang an antiphonal chant to Christ, as to a god".

It is said that by A.D. 60 there were a hundred thousand Greeks in the Church for every Jew who was a Christian. Many of the Greek Christians in Asia Minor read the Scriptures in Septuagint, the Greek version, and had separate Synagogues. The time had come to formulate the meaning of Christ and Christianity in a way that the Hellenist Jews could understand, whatever their background of thought, and this formulation had to be acceptable to the Christian Jews.

This Greek word, Logos, brought together in its meanings all that had been used to express the Wisdom of God. When used of Christ it represented and transcended the conception of the Egyptian Ptah, the Egyptian Thoth, Hermes Trismegistus, and the Wisdom which inspired Jewish writers in the later Books of the Old Testament.

The idea of the Messiah did not enter into the thinking of the Greeks, but they, like the Hermetic Teachers, could conceive of the invisible Mind of God, His creative Reason, which controls the order of the Universe. This had been the teaching of Heracleitus in the 6th century B.C. He taught: "All things happen according to the Logos". Further, he believed that the Logos dwelt in every man, "as the judge of truth, what we call Conscience, that makes it possible for Man to choose between Good and Evil:". Heracleitus lived in Ephesus where the tradition of his teaching still continued when St.John came to formulate his Gospel. Pythagoras accepted this conception of the Logos which corresponded with what he had found in Egypt where he underwent a long training in the Mysteries, and his philosophy found expression in the teaching of Socrates as presented by

Plato. The Stoics also later believed that "the Logos pervades all things."

The conception of the Logos as the Word was comprehensible to the Jews, who believed in the power of the spoken word. The Old Testament tells us much about the power of the Word of God but it is not always recognizable in translation. In Psalm 33 it is said: "By the Word of God the Heavens were made". In the Second Book of Esdras, VI: "Thy word was a perfect work." At the time of Christ very few Jews could read the Old Testament in Hebrew, as most of them now spoke Aramic, so the Scriptures were translated into Aramic and these versions were called Targums. In the Targums the Word of God (memra) was substituted for the Name of God in order to avoid the appearance of anthropomorphism. The phrase "the Word of God" occurs 320 times in the Targums, and in all the passages where it occurs the impression given is quite different from that of the original passage in the Hebrew Old Testament. For instance, the passage in Isaiah XLVIII:13, "Mine hand hath laid the foundation of the earth; and my right hand hath spanned the heavens," is rendered "By my Word I have founded the earth; and by my strength I have hung up the heavens". Deut. IX:3 becomes "*The Word of God* is a consuming fire". In Exodus XIX:17 "Moses brought forth the people out of the camp to meet with God" becomes..."to meet the Word of God". Thus the Jews were prepared to receive the idea that the Word of God had created the Universe and Man. Indeed, in the Book of Proverbs, they were familiar with the passage: "The Lord of Wisdom hath founded the earth; by understanding hath He established the heavens", Prov.III:19. And in The Wisdom of Solomon Wisdom is described as the artificer of all things, the breath of the power of God and in IX there is the following prayer:

> "O God of my fathers, and Lord of mercy, who hast made all things with Thy Word, and ordained man through Thy Wisdom...."

During the first half of the first century A.D., Philo of Alexandria, who was in touch with all the religions and philosophies of the time, had formulated the current beliefs. He was not a Christian, as far as is known, but what he wrote about the Hermetic and Greek traditions is almost an expression in Christian terms. Perhaps the most memorable and illuminating of the definitions of the Logos which he quotes are the following:

> "It is moreover, as it were, a coriander seed. For agriculturists declare that the seed of the coriander can be divided and dissected infinitely, and that every single part and section when sown comes up just as the whole seed. Such is also the Logos of God, profitable in its entirety and in every part, however small it be."
>
> "It is the Continuing Reason (Logos) of God, like the dew, encircling it on all sides, and suffering no part of it to be without its share of it. But this Reason is not apparent everywhere, but only in the man who is destitute of passions and vices; yea, subtle is it for the mind to distinguish, or to be distinguished by the mind, exceedingly translucent and pure for sight to see."
>
> "May not this Logos also be likened to the pupil of the eye? For just as the eye's pupil, though the smallest part, does yet behold all the zones of things existing – the boundless sea, and vastness of the air, and all of the whole heaven which the sun doth bound from east to west – so is the sight of the Divine Logos the keenest sight of all, so that it can behold all things; by which men shall behold

what could be more bright or more far-seeing than Logos Divine, by shining in which the other lights drive out all mist and darkness, striving to blend themselves with the soul's light."

"Who is it that poureth forth the sacred measures of true joy, if not the Cup-Bearer of God, the Logos, who is Master of the Feast."

"Therefore let God announce his good tidings to the soul in image: 'Man shall not live by bread alone, but by every word that proceedeth out of the mouth of God' – that is, he shall be nourished by the whole of Logos and by every part of it."

"The Divine Logos is further figured as a true 'Person', the Mediator between God and Man ... He the Logos ever is Himself the suppliant unto the Incorruptible on mortal kind's behalf in its distress, and is the King's ambassador to subject nature."

"He will not rend His garments – for the Logos of That-which-is, being the bond of all things, as hath been said, both holds together all the parts, and binds them, and does not suffer them to be dissolved or separated."

CHAPTER THREE

JOHN THE BAPTIST

"In the beginning was the Word, and the Word was with God, and the Word was God. The same was in the beginning with God. All things were made by him; and without him was not any thing made that was made. In him was life; and the life was the light of men. And the light shineth in darkness; and the darkness comprehended it not."

(*John* I:1-5)

CLEMENT OF ALEXANDRIA called the Fourth Gospel the Gospel of the Spirit. The writer of this Gospel unfolds the spiritual meaning of what the Synoptics record. St.John begins with the mysterious words *en arche* translated in the Authorized Version, "in the beginning", but really meaning "in principle", *in principio*, as they rendered in the Vulgate. Here is the very source, the origin of God, the Cause of all Things, the *Light*, and Christ is described as *the Word*, co-existent with God, the true Light which lighteth every man, and that if it is kindled a man can be re-born spiritually and attain eternal life. Then he may live as Jesus did. All the teaching is to this end, that we may recognize how Jesus reflected the love of the Father, and did the Will of the Father, demonstrating through the power of the Father that those who through Re-birth follow His Way of Life may tread the same path which leads to At-one-ment.

"There was a man sent from God, whose name was John. The same for a witness, to bear witness of the Light, that all men through him might believe. He was not that Light, but was sent to bear witness of that Light."

(*John* I:6-8)

John The Baptist came as a witness to testify to the light. The writer of the Gospel judges this to be so important that he announces it now at the beginning. Before Man can be aware of the light that is in him he needs to be told that it exists. He needs to understand through his mind. Before the mind of Man was developed he was intuitive but as his power of thought increased his intuitive faculty faded, so that now he has to receive through his mind knowledge of his own possibilities. There has to be within Man's mind a witness to shew him what is happening psychologically. John the Baptist is the Forerunner within a man who prepares him for re-birth. John proclaims: "He comes after me, but takes rank before me, for before I was born he already was." When the priests ask John who he is he can give no answer save the words of the prophet Isaiah: "I am a voice crying aloud in the wilderness, 'Make the Lord's highway straight.' " When a man is in the wilderness of himself, he may be able to hear an inner voice telling him to make a straight path towards the centre of himself.

In the Greek Mysteries the stages of training represent stages in the development of the candidates. There is an early stage where they are taught by one called the hydrophant, the Baptist, when they are trained in self-knowledge, they are trained so that they may recognize the revelation of light in themselves when it comes. John the Baptist in the Gospels plays this part. Readers have been puzzled by his denial of his identity when asked by the Pharisees who he was, in view of the later words of Jesus: "This is Elias, who was to come." But he may well have been moved by the spirit of the prophet, or he may even have been the reincarnation of Elijah, without knowing it. What he knew was the destiny that he had been sent to fulfil.

"The next day John seeth Jesus coming unto him, and saith, 'Behold the Lamb of God, which taketh away the sin of the world. This is he of whom I said, After me cometh a man which is preferred before me: for he was before me. And I knew him not: but that he should be made manifest to Israel, therefore am I come baptizing with water'."

It is only in the Fourth Gospel and in the Book of Revelation that Jesus is called the Lamb of God. John designates him as a sin-offering. Further he repeats: "Before I was born, he already was." The reason why Christ was able to cleanse the world of sin was because He was from God in Eternity, from the highest level, and had not shared the Fall of Man. His blood was the purest energy which could cleanse the impure bloodstream of men. John says clearly: "The very reason why I came, baptizing in water, was that he might be revealed to Israel."

He is able to see the Holy Spirit and to recognize Christ by this sign. And it is he who said once again the following day as Jesus passed by, "Behold the Lamb of God", and this brought some of those who were to be disciples into contact with Him.

The Jews had a belief that Elijah, the Prophet, would appear to herald the Messiah, and this was why the empty chair and the fifth of wine were always part of the Passover Feast. St.John in writing his Gospel makes clear that he knew that the coming of the Prophet to herald the Messiah was being enacted. This was why the Jews asked John the Baptist if he were Elijah.

Later, in Chapter III, we read that John was baptizing at Ainon near Salem, and that Jesus also was baptizing in Judea. When John's disciples were disputing this they asked him about Jesus and his answer is recorded thus:

"John answered and said, 'A man can receive nothing, except it be given him from heaven. Ye yourselves bear me witness, that I said, I am not the Christ, but that I am sent before him. He that hath the bride is the bridegroom: but the friend of the bridegroom, which standeth and heareth him, rejoiceth greatly because of the bridegroom's voice; this my joy therefore is fulfilled. He must increase, but I must decrease. He that cometh from above is above all. And what he hath seen and heard, that he testifieth; and no man receiveth his testimony. He that hath received his testimony hath set to his seal that God is true. For he whom God hath sent speaketh the words of God: for God giveth not the Spirit by measure unto him. The Father loveth the Son, and hath given all things into his hand. He that believeth on the Son hath everlasting life: and he that believeth not the Son shall not see life; but the wrath of God abideth on him'."

(*John* III:27-36)

Here is his testimony once again: "I am not the Messiah; I have been sent as his forerunner..."

It is a mysterious saying: "As he grows greater, I must grow less". The Rev. William Barclay, commenting on the presentation of John the Baptist in this Gospel, suggests that his insistence on the supremacy of Jesus in the conversations recorded in chapters one, three and four, had been made necessary by certain tendencies which had appeared in recent years among groups of Jews to raise the Baptist to the level of Jesus. Thus the note sounded in the Prologue is echoed from time to time proclaiming John the Baptist as the Forerunner, representing psychologically a certain development in a man which prepares the way for re-birth.

"I am not the Christ, but that I am sent before him." The profound implication is that the understanding which makes it possible to recognize the Christ in ourselves when He is revealed is needed less and less as the spiritual power of the New Man in Christ grows. Then there is the testimony that Christ comes from above.

❧

CHAPTER FOUR

JORDAN

IN THE first chapter of the Gospel of St.John we read that John the Baptist was baptizing in Jordan. The name "Jordan" means a "going down" and the River Jordan appears in the Jewish and Christian Scriptures as a symbol of the stream of generation flowing downwards in which the natural man is carried along. The legend that at the place where Jesus was baptized by John the Baptist the river flowed backwards signifies the power of Baptism by Water and the Spirit to make it possible for man to be re-born, so that he ascends the Path of Regeneration. It was said that a wooden Cross was erected at the place where Jesus entered the water and the Holy Spirit in the form of a Dove descended upon him. Christ represented the Wood in the Water, the Fire in the Water, the Light in the Water, for His Baptism was shewing the spiritual possibility of being born from above, and it is to this that He refers when he says to Nicodemus: "Except a man be born of water and the Spirit, he cannot enter into the Kingdom of God" (*John* III:5). From the moment of His Baptism Christ enacts the life of a man who has undergone re-birth. he is called by John the Baptist the Lamb of God, and His sacrifice begins. Thus Jordan is once more made memorable as the scene of a turning point, a reversal, and the New Testament completes what had been heralded in the Old Testament.

It is Chapter XIII of Genesis that the narrative tells us that: "Lot choose the plain of Jordan". Lot represents a part of Abram, his outer man (Abram is not yet Abraham). He goes up out of Egypt with Abram, but:

"the land was not able to bear them, that they might dwell together: for their substance was so great that they could not dwell together."

There is a quarrel amongst their herdsmen. Finally a separation takes place:

"And Abram said unto Lot, 'Let there be no strife, I pray thee, between me and thee, and between my herdmen and thy herdmen; for we be brethren. Is not the whole land before thee? Separate thyself, I pray thee, from me: if thou wilt take the left hand, then I will go to the right; or thou depart to the right hand, then I will go to the left'. And Lot lifted up his eyes, and beheld all the plain of Jordan, that it was well watered everywhere, before the Lord destroyed Sodom and Gomorrah, even as the garden of the Lord, like the land of Egypt, as thou comest unto Zoar. Then Lot chose him all the plain of Jordan; and Lot journeyed East: and they separated themselves one from the other. Abram dwelled in the land of Canaan, and Lot dwelled in the cities of the plain, and pitched his tent towards Sodom."

(*Genesis* XIII:8-12)

The outer man is now separated from the inner man. The outer man, Lot, is said to settle in the plain of Jordan, watered by the downward flowing stream of generation. The inner man stays on the high ground and receives God's blessing on his seed, for all those of the Jewish race who are re-born are called Children of Abraham. In the Book of Joshua, the third and fourth chapters describe the crossing of the river Jordan by the Children of Israel with the Ark of the Covenant. Joshua (whose name means Jesus) had been chosen to lead the Israelites into the Promised Land after the death of Moses. Joshua instructs the priests who are to bear the

Ark to stand still in Jordan. Then the procession sets out to cross the river, the people following the priests with the Ark. As the priests set foot in Jordan a great miracle comes to pass:

> "As they that bare the Ark were come unto Jordan, and the feet of the priests that bare the Ark were dipped in the brim of the water....the waters that came down from above stood and rose up upon and heap very far from the city Adam that is beside Zaretan: and those that came down toward the sea of plain, even the salt sea, failed, and were cut off: and the people passed over right against Jericho. And the priests that bare the Ark of the Covenant of the Lord stood firm on dry ground in the midst of Jordan, and all the Israelites passed over on dry ground, until all the people were passed clean over Jordan."
>
> (*Joshua* III:15:17)

This represents the stage where all that is in a man which can follow what is holiest in him can be lifted up so that it goes in a new direction. The tide of generation is stayed, and it is possible to go against the stream, against the desires of natural man, to stand dry-shod among the waters, which is one of the signs of the New Man. For Joshua stands for the New man who can preserve what is holy and lead all that looks inwards to a new dwelling-place. This is the crossing over, marked by twelve stones as a memorial to Gilgal (which means a circle – and a circle is a place where God is present).

Naaman the Syrian was cured of his leprosy by washing seven times in Jordan when he brought himself at last after much reluctance to obey the commands of Elisha. He had gone against himself, his pride, in obedience to something higher. The waters of Jordan were parted once more at the ascent of Elijah into heaven. It is said that when the time came for his departure from earth Elijah took Elisha with him and came to the river. "And Elijah took his mantle, and wrapped it together, and smote the waters, and they were divided hither and thither, so that they two went over on dry ground." Elisha's last request of his master is that a double portion of his spirit may fall upon him and he is told that this will be granted if he sees Elijah go. It is a very ancient tradition that those who are present at the transition of a holy man may receive some of his powers if they *can* receive them.

> "And it came to pass, as they still went on, And talked, that, behold, there appeared a chariot of fire, and parted them both asunder; and Elijah went up by a whirlwind into heaven. And Elisha saw it, and he cried, 'My father, my father, the chariot of Israel and the horsemen thereof'. And he saw him no more: and he took hold of his own clothes, and rent them in two pieces. He took up also the mantle of Elijah that fell from him and went back, and stood by the bank of Jordan. And he took the mantle of Elijah that fell from him and smote the waters, and said, 'Where is the Lord of Elijah?' And when he also had smitten the waters, they parted hither and thither; and Elisha went over."
>
> (II *Kings* II:11-14)

The chariot of fire is a known symbol for the Glorious Resurrection of the body, in which Elijah would have ascended. For Elisha this is a stage of crossing-over, first in the power given by his master, and then in the power which he had received and was able to use. It was on the bank of Jordan that John the Baptist first appeared in the Gospel of John, of whom later Christ said: "If ye will receive it, this is Elias, which was to come'. John himself denied this, when questioned by the people, but it was likely that in descending to earth to play the part of the

Forerunner he was separated in his mind from his memory. Elijah was taken up in the chariot of fire on the banks of Jordan, and John re-appeared in the same place. This suggests that a connection was to be pointed out in the Scriptures for those who had eyes to read. A sacred place referred to in the Scriptures has always the significance of a place in one's psychology. It is after the Baptism in Jordan, signifying re-birth, that Jesus is represented in the Gospel of John as gathering His disciples together. Once more in the course of His ministry He was to return to the place of Baptism. This was when He had been attacked by the Jews at the Feast of Dedication in Jerusalem. His retirement to the place of re-birth preceded the miracle of the Raising of Lazarus.

Jacob's Well

Again here is a psychological place referred to in the Scriptures as being the scene of certain events. It is at this Well that Jesus asks the Woman of Samaria: "Give me to drink". Here he tells her of the Living Water that he can give which "shall be in a man a well of water springing up into everlasting life." And he tells her that he is the Messiah. Because he has told her the truth about her own life she believes him also in this and spreads the news so that the people of Samaria testify "that this is indeed Christ, the Saviour of the World". Maurice Nicoll interprets this encounter psychologically as the awakening of the woman's soul, for after being turned to the five senses (which her five husbands represent) she has come to the Well – she is now open to new Truth. This was the same Well where Jacob rolled away the stone which had been blocking psychological understanding, as

Nicoll describes it. When the stone was rolled back the flock could be watered. This event signifies an opening of the mind to the source of new understanding above the literal level. The name of the Well, Jacob's Well, gives the key to the meaning of the mysterious conversation between Jesus and the Samaritan woman. She is the Soul which is so far a stranger to the man, as the Samaritans were to the Jews. And this strange new Soul can accept the reality of Christ.

CHAPTER FIVE

THE SIX SIGNS

Water into Wine

THE DISCIPLES stand for the twelve powers in the Perfect Man through which He will ultimately transmit His teaching. Once the disciples are assembled the Signs of Christ begin to be manifested. In the Gospel of John these form an octave.

The first sign is not recorded in the Synoptic Gospels. It derives from the Greek Mysteries. In the Greek Mystery Schools where Demeter was worshipped a ceremony of marriage was celebrated on the third day which was witnessed by the candidate. This was psychologically the marriage of Good and Truth, of the Heart and Mind. Much preparation and training must have preceded this. Six stages are indicated. Jesus Himself is the candidate. Cana of Galilee is no known place, but Galilee is said to mean the Circle of Eternity and "this beginning of Signs" is an eternal happening. After the six stages of development in Man, as in the evolution of the Universe, the seventh is the culmination and the seventh stage operates from within, so that there is a transformation of the whole, of all that has gone before. The six stone water pots represent work on one level, all the work that has been done "in the manner of purifying the Jews", work towards purifying up to a certain point. Up to this point the candidate has gradually been withdrawn from the influence of the Mother, what is earthly in Himself. It is there that Christ rejects his Mother: "Woman, what have I to do with thee?" He turns from the natural good to divine goodness, which floods the whole being of a man at this stage and this is expressed in parable as the turning of Water into Wine, for when truth is loved from the heart there is a marriage. And in this narrative there is a hint of what lies ahead: "Mine hour is not yet come". Is the Wine an indication of the power of the Heart's blood which will redeem the world?

The Healing of the Nobleman's Son

The second Sign is demonstrated also in Cana of Galilee some time afterwards where Jesus has returned after being in Jerusalem and Samaria. This is the first of the healing miracles, all of which represent psychological healing in that they contribute towards making the person whole. Here a child is made whole. The nobleman's son is healed in absence when the fever leaves him at *the seventh hour*. It might be said that someone sick of fever is sick of self-love which feverishly seeks its own will. This miracle and the next shew the power of Christ in a man to heal all psychological discord.

The Healing at the Pool of Bethesda

The third Sign is shewn in Jerusalem by the Pool of Bethesda, having five porches. Bethesda means "House of Mercy". This, like the first miracle, occurs only in the Fourth Gospel. The healing takes place on the Sabbath, as in many of the examples of healing in the Synoptic Gospels.

> "And a certain man was there, which had an infirmity thirty and eight years. When Jesus saw him lie; and knew that he had been now a long time in that case, he saith unto

> him: 'Wilt thou be made whole?' The impotent man answered him, 'Sir, I have no man, when the water is troubled, to put me into the pool: but while I am coming, another steppeth down before me'. Jesus saith unto him, 'Rise, take up thy bed and walk'. And immediately the man was made whole, and took up his bed, and walked: and on the same day was the sabbath."
>
> (*John* V:5-9)

The period of time, thirty-eight years during which the man has lain powerless to take the step that will heal him, is interesting, The number thirty-eight is so close to thirty-nine, a number of completion; three implies completion (threefold) and nine transformation, three times three. And thirteen is a mystic number in which Christ Himself is present, with the Twelve. What is important in this healing is that Christ speaks to the impotent man and asks him: "Wouldst thou be made whole?" Maurice Nicoll describes his disease as "the disease of higher Truth being paralysed by lower truth", and says that this disease makes him psychologically halt, lame and withered. When he meets with Christ (in himself) and hears the command, "Take up thy bed and walk", he is able to obey the Higher Will which is now operating in him. This impotence or inertia is the disease of every man who reaches a certain point in his development. It is a cosmic influence which pulls a man down when he seeks to ascend and only a shock can then raise him to the next state. He cannot go further until he hears the voice of Christ in himself. Such a miracle could be enacted only on the Sabbath which is the period of time in which a man rests from his external self and is in the place where he can hear the voice that commands him and gives him energy to do what is commanded. Later,

Jesus meeting him, says: "Behold, thou art made whole: sin no more lest a worse thing come unto thee." This is a very important occasion in the Gospel narrative because it is said afterwards: "And therefore did the Jews persecute Jesus, and sought to slay him, because he had done these things on the Sabbath day" (John V:16). The Jews represent literal truth which seeks to destroy spiritual truth, being blind to the inner meaning of the Sabbath which Moses taught long before, and hating what they cannot understand. Christ brings events to a head consciously at this point when He says: "My Father worketh hitherto and I work". The Jews then have double cause, as they think, to seek to slay Him because He said also that God was His Father, making Himself equal with God.

The Miracle of the Feeding of the Five Thousand

This sign is described in the Synoptic Gospels but only in the Fourth Gospel is it said that it was a small boy who had the bread and that the loaves were of barley. This miracle is enacted to shew the people the never-failing source of the energy of consciousness that is available to them. The number 5 is a prime number. Man composed of the 4 elements, can be completed only by the awakening of a 5th element in him, the quintessence, the spiritualizing element. The symbol of the pentagram is itself a symbol of healing, or making whole. The two fish are the Two Fish in the glyph of Pisces, the Sign of Christ.

The multitude in this parable rest on the grass, the green place in the barren desert, which has been watered so that it becomes a place of new growing life. The loaves are distributed to the people by the disciples. It is their task to transmit what they receive to others. Twelve baskets remain after all have been fed. There is one substance which increases as you use it – energy of consciousness. Twelve, the number of the Zodiac, denotes completion in space. There is enough for all, for the 12 types of Man, corresponding with the 12 disciples. This parable illustrates once for all that Christ is the source of consciousness and that if the small amount of consciousness that a man has within, as a gift, is used, he can receive enough to sustain the whole man.

The Miracle of Walking on the Waters

> "When Jesus therefore perceived that they would come and take him by force, to make him a king, he departed again into a mountain himself alone. And when even was now come, his disciples went down unto the sea, and entered into a ship, and went over the sea toward Caparnaum. And it was now dark, and Jesus was not come to them. And the sea arose by reason of a great wind that blew. So when they had rowed about five and twenty or thirty furlongs, they see Jesus walking on the sea, and drawing nigh unto the ship: and they were afraid. But he saith unto them: 'It is I; be not afraid'. Then they willingly received him into the ship: and immediately the ship was at the land wither they went.
>
> (*John* VI:15-21)

It was after the miracle of the feeding of the five thousand that Christ walked on the waters of the Sea of Galilee, shewing that He could walk on the waters of life. This is the fifth Sign. Without His presence the disciples were tossed about in their boat on the waves. But when they were aware that Christ was present, and heard His words: "*Ego Eimi*" – "It is I" – their fear was dispelled and they were immediately taken where they wanted to go. This is again an eternal experience that is described, taking place within the Circle of Eternity. When a man's consciousness is araised so that he is aware of the approaching Presence, it is the I, the Real I, which takes over, and the waves are stilled, the fear cast out, and the Master directs the course. The multitude now seek Jesus and find him at Capernaum. It is here that He tells them: "I am the bread of life: he that cometh to me shall never hunger and he that believeth on me shall never thirst". He is trying to teach them what He can give if they will only ask for it. The bread of life is the symbol of this energy of consciousness, which is inexhaustible, as the saints have found when they have drawn upon it to do what is impossible to their own strength.

The comment made by Jesus, "Ye seek me, not because ye saw the miracles, but because ye did eat of the loaves, and were filled", may mean that because the people had once been nourished by this bread they were moved to seek the Giver again. They were not necessarily seeking sensation after witnessing a miracle.

In the Fourth Gospel there is not the same account of the Last Supper as in the Synoptic Gospels. There is no trace of laying down a ritual to be enacted. But in this Gospel there is interpretation of the meaning of the bread that Christ offers to those who can receive it, the substance which is Himself, His consciousness, which can transform a man, so that his whole substance is changed, so that after death he can inhabit his immortal body, the Body of Resurrection. All this is implied in the words: "This is the bread of life which cometh down from heaven, that a man may eat thereof and not die...I am the living bread which came down from heaven; if any man eat of this bread he shall live for ever: and the bread that I will give is my flesh, which I will give for the life of the world". "Flesh" in the *New Testament* is a technical word meaning the psychology of a man, not the body. Thus it is that "flesh' can nourish the inner bodies of a man, while "blood" can cleanse.

The Healing of the Blind Man

The sixth Sign is the Healing of the Blind Man.

> "And as Jesus passed by, he saw a man which was blind from his birth. And his disciples asked him, saying, 'Master, who did sin, this man, or his parents, that he was born blind?' Jesus answered, 'Neither hath this man sinned, nor his parents: but that the words of God should be made manifest in him. I must work the works of him that sent me, while it is day: the night cometh, when no man can work. As long as I am in the world, I am the light of the world.' When he had thus spoken, he spat on the ground, and made clay of the spittle, and he anointed the eyes of the blind man with the clay. And he said unto him, 'Go, wash in the pool of Siloam,' (which is by interpretation, Sent). he went his way therefore and washed, and came seeing."
>
> (*John* IX:1-7)

Here it is quite plainly stated that the miracle was done for a certain purpose, "that the works of God should be made manifest in him". The man is playing a part although he does not know it. The question of the disciples is interesting. They thought that perhaps he was paying for some wrong done in the past, that blindness was his Karma. The answer also is interesting. His blindness from birth had been allotted to him in his fate so that Jesus might cure him to shew the power of God. He was told to wash in the pool of Siloam. Siloam means an outlet of water, and the pool is filled from a spring issuing from the sacred Mount Moriah. When he was asked whether the eighteen, upon whom the Tower of Siloam fell, were sinners above all men that dwelt in Jerusalem, Jesus answered: "Nay: but except ye repent, ye shall all likewise perish". He implied that the manner of death was not important, but only those who had undergone metanoia, change of mind, could have the gift of eternal life. Each cure is done in a different way. On this occasion Jesus mingles His spittle with the clay of the earth and anoints the blind eyes. Surely this is a mingling of the divine and earthly, symbolizing the insight that a man can have when he encounters Christ in himself.

This miracle likewise took place on the Sabbath, and the reason for the miracle is given in verses 39-41:

> "And Jesus said, 'For judgement I am come into the world, that they which see not might see; and that they which see might be made blind'. And some of the Pharisees which were with him heard these words, and said unto him, 'Are we blind also?' Jesus said unto them, 'If ye were blind, ye should have no sin: but now ye say, We see; therefore your sin remaineth'."

Thus it can be understood that the purpose of the healing was to shew that only through the power of Christ can we really see – with the inner eye, sometimes called by mystics "the eye of eternity". We cannot really see with the outer eye. Insight only comes when a man has developed a new sense, an inner sense, which can shew him what is within. We are all blind until our inner sense (insight) is developed, but we can be made to see. The

Pharisees could not gain insight because they thought that they could already see.

The Pharisees had even now given one more example of their inner blindness when they said: "This man is not of God, because he keepeth not the Sabbath-day". They were blind to the inner meaning of the Sabbath which would have shewn them that it was a day for healing, for making whole.

CHAPTER SIX

THE RAISING OF LAZARUS

Lazarus is really Everyman. He is described in his sisters' words as "he whom thou lovest". Lazarus is the man whom Jesus loved, and therefore he is every human being. Thus we are told that this miracle is about ourselves, and what is possible for us. In this miracle the whole task of Jesus is summarized: to awaken those who are asleep, or dead, in life. He said: "Our friend Lazarus sleepeth; but I go that I may awake him out of sleep."

"Now a certain man was sick, named Lazarus, of Bethany, the town of Mary and her sister Martha. (It was that Mary which anointed the Lord with ointment, and wiped his feet with her hair, whose brother Lazarus was sick.) Therefore his sisters sent unto him, saying: 'Lord, behold, he whom thou lovest is sick.' When Jesus heard that, he said, 'This sickness is not unto death, but for the glory of God, that the Son of God might be glorified thereby'. Now Jesus loved Martha, and her sister, and Lazarus. When he had heard therefore that he was sick, he abode two days still in the same place where he was. Then after that saith he to his disciples, 'Let us go to Judea again.' His disciples say unto him, 'Master, the Jews of late sought to stone thee; and goest thou thither again?' Jesus answered, 'Are there not twelve hours in a day? If any man walk in the day, he stumbleth not, because he seeth the light of this world. But if a man walk in the night he stumbleth, because there is no light in him.' These things said he: and after that he saith unto them, 'Our friend Lazarus sleepeth: but I go, that I may awake him out of sleep, he shall do well'. Howbeit Jesus spake of his death" but they thought that he had spoken of taking of rest in sleep. Then said Jesus unto them plainly, 'Lazarus is dead.

And I am glad for your sakes that I was not there, to the intent ye may believe; nevertheless let us go unto him'. Then said Thomas, which is called had spoken of taking of rest in sleep. Then said Jesus unto them plainly, 'Lazarus is dead. And I am glad for your sakes that I was not there, to the intent ye may believe; nevertheless let us go unto him'. Then said Thomas, which is called Didymus, unto his fellow disciples, 'Let us also go that we may die with him'. Then when Jesus came, he found that he had lain in the grave four days already."

(*John* XI:1-17)

Lazarus had been in the grave four days when Jesus came. It is clearly indicated that Jesus delayed His coming, in order that the death should be shewn as being complete before he worked the miracle. The number 4, the number of the elements, is the number of Man on earth unawakened by the fifth element, the quintessence, which gives life to the spiritual man. And there is also a tradition that the etheric body may not become disentangled from the body before the fourth day.

"Now Bethany was nigh unto Jerusalem, about fifteen furlongs off: and many of the Jews came to Martha and Mary, to comfort them concerning their brother. Then Martha, as soon as she heard that Jesus was coming, went and met him: but Mary sat still in the house. Then said Martha unto Jesus, 'Lord, if thou hadst been here, my brother had not died. But I know, that even now, whatsoever thou wilt ask of God, God will give it thee'. Jesus saith unto her, "Thy brother shall rise again'. Martha said unto him, 'I know that he shall rise again in the resurrection at the last day'. Jesus said unto her, 'I am the resurrection, and the life: he that believeth in me, though he were dead, yet he shall live: And whosoever liveth and believeth in me shall never die. Believest thou this? She saith unto him 'Yes, Lord: I believe that thou art the Christ, the Son of God, which should come into the world'. And when she had so said, she went her way, and called Mary her sister secretly, unto him 'Yes, Lord: I believe that thou art the Christ, the Son of God, which should come into the world'. And when she had so said, she went her way, and called Mary her sister secretly, saying, 'The Master is come, and calleth for thee'. As soon as she heard that she arose quickly, and came unto him. Now Jesus was not yet come into the town, but was in that place where Martha met him. The Jews then which were with her in the house, and comforted her, when they saw Mary, that she rose up hastily and went out, followed her, saying, 'She goeth unto the grave to weep there'. Then when Mary was come where Jesus was, and saw him, she fell down at his feet, saying unto him, 'Lord, if thou hadst been here, my brother had not died.' When Jesus therefore saw her weeping, and the Jews also weeping which came with her, he groaned in the spirit and was troubled. And said, 'Where have ye laid him?' They said unto him 'Lord, come and see.' Jesus wept."

(*John* XI:18-35)

Martha, representing the outer, practical affection, goes to meet Jesus, "but Mary sat still in the house". The Soul looking outwards says: "Lord, if thou hadst been here my brother had not died". The same words are spoken by Mary, The Soul looking inwards, but Mary falls weeping at the feet of Jesus when she speaks the words, and then we are told, Jesus wept. It seems he weeps out of Divine Compassion not because Lazarus is physically dead but because Man who he loves is dead in life.

"Jesus therefore again groaning in himself cometh to the grave. It was a cave, and a stone lay upon it. Jesus said, 'Take away the stone'. Martha the sister of him that was dead, saith unto him, 'Lord by this time he stinketh: for he hath been dead four days'. Jesus saith unto her, 'Said I not unto thee, that, if thou wouldest believe, thou shouldest see the glory of God?' Then they took away the stone from the place where the dead was they took away the stone from the place where the dead was laid. And Jesus lifted up his eyes, and said, 'Father, I thank thee that thou hast heard me. And I knew that thou hearest me always: but because of the people which stand by I said it, that they may believe that thou hast sent me'. And when he had thus spoken, he cried out with a loud voice, 'Lazarus, come forth'. And he that was dead came forth, bound hand and foot with graveclothes; and his face was bound with a napkin, Jesus saith unto them, "Loose him, and let him go'."

(*John* XI:38-44)

When they go to the grave Martha reminds them that Lazarus has been dead four days, and that the body will have begun to decay. This is said perhaps to stress the miraculous event which is about to take place. And once more Jesus says that what is to be done is for the glory of God, and that His Father has heard His prayer, whereupon the resounding command rings out: "Lazarus, come forth". This is the command that is given to Man asleep when the moment comes for him to awaken from his sleep, his living death, and stand erect in his own being in the power of Christ working through Him. The name Lazarus means "whom God has aided".

This miracle would seem to be a foreshadowing of Christ's Resurrection. The body lies in the grave, the stone is rolled in front of it. If those who witnessed the miracle could have remembered the words of Jesus:

"Verily, verily I say unto you, the Son can do nothing of himself, but what he seeth the Father do: for what things soever he doeth, these also doeth the Son likewise. For the Father loveth the Son, and sheweth him all things that himself doeth: and he will shew him greater works than

> these, that ye may marvel. For as the Father raiseth up the dead and quickeneth them; even so the Son quickeneth whom he will."
>
> (*John* V:19-21)

Before their eyes these words have been fulfilled: "As the Father raiseth up the dead and quickeneth them; even so the Son quickeneth whom he will". Jesus has raised Lazarus. How much more will the Father be able to raise His Son when He lies in the tomb. This whole passage in the fifth chapter of St.John is a wonderful prophecy, not of the resurrection at the end of the world, but of the regeneration of Man now in his life. These last miracles have been arranged consciously to manifest the glory of God. The Raising of Lazarus has the effect of precipitating the action of the priests against Him. A strange comment is made by them: "If we let him thus alone, all men will believe on him: and the Romans shall come and take away both our place and nation". This is followed by the prophecy of Caiaphas which is recorded only in the Fourth Gospel:

> "Ye know nothing at all, nor consider that it is expedient for us, that one man should die for the people, and that the whole nation perish not."
>
> (*John* XI:50)

The Gospel writer interprets this as a prophecy that Jesus should die for the nation, and for all "the children of God that were scattered abroad". Further, the Evangelist indicates that this prophecy was given to Caiaphas to speak, in that God spoke through His High Priest.

We now read that Jesus withdrew to a city called Ephraim near the wilderness. Ephraim means "fruitfulness". It was a period of preparation for what was shortly to come, and this lasted until six days before Passover when He came once more to Bethany, and supped with Martha and Mary and Lazarus. This was the time when Mary anointed His feet with costly spikenard and He said that it was for the day of His burying. St.John recalls the fragrance: "The house was filled with the odour of the ointment". Once again the six stages of preparation are presented to us, having begun with the Supper at Bethany and the Anointing, on the first day. Then the journey to Jerusalem takes place, as in the Synoptic Gospels. Fulfilling the prophecy, "Behold, thy King cometh, sitting on an ass's colt", he rode into Jerusalem. The name in the East given to an ass's colt was "the Son of a Virgin, and the ass was a symbol of the physical body. The Evangelist points out that the disciples afterwards remembered the prophecies and saw how they were fulfilled, but not at the time.

And now, in this Gospel only, comes the final link with the Greek Mysteries through the disciples with the Greek names, where it is related that certain Greeks came to Philip, Philip tells Andrew, and Jesus describes the meaning of his Death and Resurrection in Greek terms: "Except a corn of wheat fall into the ground and die, it abideth alone: but if it die, it bringeth forth much fruit". And only in this Gospel the voice from Heaven is heard that the people thought to be the voice of an angel and Jesus said: "The voice came not because of me but for your sakes". Again comes the insistence on light: "Yet a little while is the light with you", and "I am come a light into the world, that whosoever believeth on me should not abide in darkness".

CHAPTER SEVEN

THE LAST SUPPER

IN THE FOURTH GOSPEL the Last Supper is not the Feast of the Passover. This is made very clear. It would seem to have been instituted as a Christian Feast. In the Synoptic Gospels however the narrative reads as though Jesus and His disciples celebrate the Passover before the appointed day. All the Evangelists agree that on the first day of unleavened bread the disciples are sent to announce Jesus' coming and to prepare the Upper Room. They are given the message in *Matthew*:

> "The Master saith, My time is at hand; I will keep the Passover at thy house with my disciples."

And we are told that in the evening they sat down to eat. St.John says nothing of this, but tells us that before the feast of the Passover, supper being ended Jesus proceeded to wash the feet of His disciples:

> "Now before the feast of the passover, when Jesus knew that his hour was come that he should depart out of this world unto the Father, having loved his own which were in the world, he loved them unto the end. And supper being ended, the devil having now put into the heart of Judas Iscariot, Simon's son, to betray him; Jesus knowing that the Father had given all things into his hands, and that he was come from God, and went to God; He riseth from supper, and laid aside his garments; and took a towel, and girded himself. After that he poureth water into a bason, and began to wash the disciples' feet, and to wipe them with the towel wherewith he was girded."
>
> (*John* XIII:1-5)

This is followed by the two prophecies concerning the disciples, Judas and Peter. Jesus says that He has chosen Judas so that the Scripture may be fulfilled and quotes *Psalm* XLI:9:

> "He who eats my bread has lifted up his heel against me."

He then makes this most significant comment, which only the New English Bible seems to render adequately:

> "I tell you this now, before the event, that when it happens you may believe that I am what I am" (literally, "I am").
>
> (*John* XIII:19)

When Judas has received the sop and gone out to do what he has to do, Jesus gives the eleven disciples the New Commandment, "Love one another as I have loved you". Peter declares that he will lay down his life for Jesus whose response is:

> "Wilt thou lay down thy life for my sake? Verily, verily, I say unto thee, the cock shall not crow, till thou hast denied me thrice."
>
> (*John* XIII:38)

At 3.00 a.m. the changing of the Roman Guard was announced by a trumpet call, which was known as gallicnium, the Latin for cockcrow of which the Greek word *alektorophonia* is a translation. (Cocks were not allowed in the Holy City.)

These prophecies belong to a series of sayings which prove that Jesus had foreknowledge. When Peter said he would lay down his life for the sake of Christ he was taken at his word, but he was not to know it yet. There is an interesting pattern in what is recorded of Peter at the end of the Fourth Gospel. It is as though the threefold denial were balanced by the threefold question, "Simon, son of Jonas, lovest thou me?" and the threefold command, "Feed my lambs".

In the words which follow, the Risen Christ gives a hint by what death He should glorify God. In the *Acts of Peter* one more denial of Christ is recorded when he fled from Rome.

> "And as he went forth of the city, he saw the Lord, entering into Rome. And when he saw him, he said: 'Lord whither goest thou thus?' And the Lord said unto him: 'I go into Rome to be crucified'. And Peter said unto him: 'Lord art thou being crucified again?' He said unto him: 'Yea, Peter, I am being crucified again'. And Peter came to himself: and having beheld the Lord ascending up into heaven, he returned to Rome rejoicing, and glorifying the Lord, for that he said: 'I am being crucified': the which was about to befall Peter."

"*Peter came to himself.*" He welcomes the Cross and asks to be crucified upside down in order to demonstrate the Fall of Man.

> "For the first man, whose race I bear in my appearance, fell head downwards... He, then being pulled down... established this whole disposition of all thing, being hanged up an image of the creation wherein he made the things of the right hand into the left hand and the left hand into the right hand, and changed about all the marks of their nature, so that he thought those things that were not fair to be fair, and those that were in truth evil to be good. Concerning which the Lord says in a mystery: 'Unless ye make the things of the right hand as those of the left, and those of the left as those of the right, and those

that are above as those below, and those that are behind as those that are before, ye shall not have knowledge of the Kingdom'."

After Jesus' prophecy of Peter's denial the long final discourse follows which seems to link heaven and earth, so that the disciples will ever afterwards remember it as an experience of eternity. Jesus speaks of Himself as the Way to the Father, and promises to prepare a place for the disciples in one of the many mansions of His Father's house. One of the Early Fathers quoted in the Philokalia interprets the "many mansions" thus:

"When the Saviour spoke of the many mansions of His Father, he meant the different degrees of mind that are given dwellings in that realm, that is the diversities and distinctions of spiritual gifts to be enjoyed according to the station of mind. For he called the mansions many, not because they are in different places, but because the difference lies in the degree of gifts. Just as each man enjoys the physical sun according to the clarity and receptive power of his sight, and as one lamp gives differing degrees of illumination in a house, although the light is not divided into many lights; so in the life to come all the righteous are indivisibly put to dwell in one realm, but each of them is illumined by the one Spiritual Sun, according to his own measure, and attracts to himself joy and gladness according to his quality, as it were from over the same air, from one place, the throne of vision and image. And no one sees the measure of his neighbour, whether he be above of below him, lest the sight of the greater grace of his neighbour and his own lack should cause him sadness and grief. There each, according to his own gift of grace, has inward joy in his own measure. But, outside them all, there is one vision and realm, and apart from the two degrees, namely, one realm on high and one below, there is between them the multiplicity of varying gifts."

In this disclosure is stressed once more the link between Jesus and the Father:

> "No man cometh unto the Father but by me. If ye had known me, ye should have known my Father also: and from henceforth ye know him and have seen him... He that hath seen me hath seen the Father."

How can the paradox be understood that "I am in the Father and the Father in me"? We know that what is highest in us is in the very centre of ourselves and we are contained in it. This is what we have to believe. What is it to believe? It is to be aware of as a certainty. How clear the instructions given are. If the disciples are aware from certain knowledge that as Christ says He does nothing of himself but God works through him, and can let what is highest in them, which is the power of Christ, work through them, then nothing will be impossible to them. He promises them that what they ask in His Name He will do.

Now He promises that the Father will send the Paraclete, the Spirit of Truth, which will dwell in them. The world cannot believe in its existence because it is invisible.

The condition of receiving the Paraclete is to love Christ and keep His commandments. This would include the New Commandment: to love one another as Christ had loved them. If they can be linked to Christ in their love and faith, they are promised that the power of the Spirit will strengthen them and bring to them remembrance and understanding of all Christ's words which they had not understood at the time when they were spoken:

"But the Comforter, which is the Holy Ghost, whom the Father will send in my name, he shall teach you all things, and bring all things to your remembrance, whatsoever I have said unto you."

(*John* XIV:26)

The Holy Ghost cannot work through them as long as they depend on Jesus' visible presence which is external to themselves. Therefore it is expedient that He leaves them.

There are four verses in Chapter XVI:8-11, which are obscurely translated in the Authorized Version, but there is a clear rendering in The New English Bible. These verses describe the power of the Paraclete, called here the Advocate:

"When he comes, he will confute the world, and shew where wrong and right and judgment lie. He will convict them of wrong, by their refusal to believe in me; he will convince them that right is on my side, by shewing that I go to the Father, when I pass from your sight and he will convince them of divine judgment, by shewing that the Prince of this world stands condemned."

Then it is said:

"Howbeit when he, the Spirit of truth, is come, he will guide you into all truth: for he shall not speak of himself; but whatsoever he shall hear, that shall he speak: and he will shew you things to come."

This prophecy was fulfilled after Pentecost when the disciples found that words were given them to speak and the power to heal. When a lame man asked alms of Peter at the gate of the Temple, Peter replied:

"Silver and gold have I none; but such as I have give I thee: In the name of Jesus Christ of Nazareth rise up and walk."

The man was healed and when the people marvelled at this, Peter told them that the healing was done "through faith in his name", the name of the Holy One who, they had killed – and he was able to proclaim afterwards the power of the Name of Jesus of Nazareth, saying:

> "This is the stone which was set at naught of you builders, which is become the head of the corner. Neither is there salvation in any other: for there is none other name under heaven given among men, whereby we must be saved."
>
> (*Acts* IV:11-12)

CHAPTER EIGHT

THE HYMN OF JESUS

In Matthew XXVI:30, the verse which follows the description of the breaking of Bread and offering of Wine, we read "And when they had sung a hymn, they went out into the Mount of Olives". There is a similar verse in Mark XIV:26, and both verses precede the avowal of Peter. Certain references to the Hymn of Jesus in other writers may refer to this.

It is likely to be the Dance of Jesus recorded in the Acts of John to which St.Augustine alludes. He quotes from the introduction of the Gnostic MS. of the Hymn: "This Hymn is not put in the Canon, because of those who think according to themselves, and not according to the Spirit and Truth of God, and that is written: 'It is good to hide the Sacrament of the King; but it is honourable to reveal the works of God'." The Hymn of Jesus and the experience of the disciple John in his subtle body when Christ speaks to him on the mountain during the Crucifixion and tells him of the meaning of the Cross are omitted from the Canon, although they had been incorporated into the Fourth Gospel they would have thrown great light on the work and teaching and power of Christ.

G.R.S.Mead thinks that the Hymn and Dance represent an initiation ceremony which would have taken place before the final initiation, the Crucifixion. The dance of the One surrounded by the disciples in a ring like the Sun encircled by his planets represents the harmony of One who is perfect. He is in tune with the Universe and with His own powers which can now go out from Him through the disciples. The dialogue states the necessity for complete experience in all things, and it contains instruction on the mystery of suffering, which, if understood would have given the disciples insight into the meaning of the Crucifixion.

When the One sings "I would be pierced and I would pierce", He is foretelling the shedding of His blood when the spear of the centurion pierces His heart, so that it may redeem the world, and He foretells also the piercing of the hearts of men by the spear of light which He wields through the power of His suffering. Christ says to each disciple:

> "Understand, by dancing, what I do; for thine is the Passion of Man that I am to suffer. Thou couldest not at all be conscious of what thou dost suffer, were I not sent as Thy Word by the Father. Seeing what I suffer, thou sawest me as suffering; and seeing, thou didst not stand, but wast moved wholly, moved to be wise."

> "If thou hadst known now to suffer, thou wouldst have power not to suffer. Know then how to suffer and thou has power not to suffer."

It is only in St.John's Gospel that the piercing of the side of Jesus after death is recorded:

> "But one of the soldiers with a spear pierced his side, and forthwith came there out blood and water. And he that saw it bare record, and his record is true; and he knoweth that he saith true, that ye might believe."
>
> (*John* XIX:34-35)

In the Synoptic Gospels the command is recorded to drink His Blood, in the Cup of Wine, but only St.John testifies to the piercing of the heart which shews how the Blood was shed.

And it is St.John who points out that a further prophecy is fulfilled here: "Again another scriptures saith: 'They shall look on him whom they pierced'."

Ritual Dances had for centuries been symbolical of treading a way that is in harmony with the Universe. Just as Christ repeated so many times that He was doing the Will of His Father – so the Dance represented that each of the twelve was to play his part in fulfilling the plan. "Who danceth not, knows not what is being done." The disciples were now being initiated in the parts that they were to play in the work of making the teaching known to the world. The music played on the seven-stringed lyre sounds the planetary harmony. "I would pipe; dance ye all...The one eight sounds with us".

Later Christ says:

> "But for Me, if thou wouldst know what I was: in a word I am the Word who did play (dance) all things, and was not shamed at all."

This was indeed the culmination of the teaching if they could have understood it then, for they were being told that everything that was to happen was the fulfilment of the Word of God. The long discourse and now this Hymn had given them this clear Truth. But they could not receive it then. The recorder of the Hymn concludes:

> "And having danced these things with us, Beloved, the Lord went forth – And we, as though beside ourselves, or wakened out of deep sleep, fled each our several ways."

It would seem that this passage in the Acts of John would have fitted in after the first verse of John XVIII, describing how Jesus and his disciples entered the garden.

At the end of the Hymn the disciples fled. What could cause them to flee except the arrival, referred to in verse 3, of the "officers from the chief priests and Pharisees" whom Judas brought to the garden?

CHAPTER NINE

THE CRUCIFIXION

THE PASSAGE OF JESUS and His disciples over the brook Cedron into the garden reminds us of David's passage over the same river in flight from Absalom:

> "And all the country wept with a loud voice and all the people passed over: the King himself also passed over the brook Kidron, and all the people passed over, towards the way of the wilderness."
>
> (II *Samuel* XVI:23)

David also wept as he ascended the Mount of Olives. It was a place of sorrow. Absalom had rebelled against him and his suffering seemed more than he could bear.

It is only in this Gospel that the brook Cedron is named. It was literally a channel into which the blood of the Temple sacrifices drained away. Thus Jesus' passage over the brook was fitting for the Lamb of God.

Only St.John speaks of Gethsemane as a *garden*. The Synoptic Gospels call it a *place*. It is as though St.John had another garden in mind, linking the Fall with the Redemption.

It is said that Jesus went forward to meet the priests and Pharisees who with Judas were coming towards him with "lanterns and torches and weapons".

> "Jesus therefore, knowing all things that should come upon him, went forth and said unto them, 'Whom seek ye?' They answereth him, 'Jesus of Nazareth'. Jesus said unto them, 'I am he'. And Judas also, which betrayed him stood with them. As soon as he had said unto them, I am he, they went backward, and fell to the ground."

There is no kiss, as in the Synoptic Gospels, but this strange sentence: *they went backward and fell to the ground*. This was at the admission of Jesus' presence. It is as though only the disciple John has seen this, Peter is rebuked for cutting off the ear of Malchus. It is not recorded here that Jesus healed the ear but that He says: "The cup which my Father hath given me, shall I not drink it?" It is said that another disciple followed Jesus when He was taken into the palace of the High Priest, the reason being that "that disciple was known unto the high priest". It is supposed that John was this disciple.

Peter's denial of being a disciple of Jesus made in the outer court is recorded and the subsequent crowing of the cock, but it is not said that he wept, as in the Synoptic Gospels.

It is explained only in St.John's Gospel that the Priests "went not into the judgement hall, lest they might eat the passover". Here is inside knowledge displayed, and with what irony is it indicated that after delivering the messiah over unto judgment they celebrated the Feast of the Passover, where they would eat lamb roasted, in memory of the lamb that was slain in Egypt to save their lives through its blood, and where the Cup of Wine awaited Elijah, the Forerunner, for whom the door was always open, in case he should enter *to announce the Coming of the Messiah*.

In St.John's Gospel more of Jesus' conversation with Pilate is disclosed than in other Gospels. Jesus makes a clear declaration about His destiny; in answer to the question: "Art thou a king then?": He says:

> "Thou sayest that I am a king. To this end was I born, for this cause came I unto the world, that I should bear witness unto the truth".
>
> (*John* XVIII:27)

It is at this point (recorded only in this Gospel) that Pilate asks his question: "What is truth?" and in the Acts of Pilate there is an interesting continuation of their talk together:

> "Pilate saith unto him: 'What is truth?' Jesus saith unto him: 'Truth is of heaven'. Pilate saith: 'Is there not truth on earth?' Jesus saith unto Pilate: 'Thou seest how they which speak the truth are judged of them that have authority upon earth'."

Pilate is now prepared to release Jesus and suggests to the people that He should be the prisoner released at the Passover, according to the custom of setting one prisoner free at the feast. The cry for the release of Barabbas, the robber, instead of Jesus, is in all the Gospels.

This cry: "*Not this man, but Barabbas*", still echoes down the ages as the choice made by Man unregenerate in his ignorance since he fell from grace.

Barabbas is a mysterious figure. Esoterically a robber is one who robs a man of his spiritual sustenance, the very gift that Jesus had offered to men. And here is one of the keys to the inner meaning of the Crucifixion, that Everyman, until he is at one with Christ in himself, serves the Robber, thus depriving himself of the spiritual energy which could work for his redemption. The Robber takes his energy and uses it for life in the world, for all that gratifies the self-will, so that the weak Inner Man who longs for Christ has no strength to overcome the world.

The scene of the scourging of Jesus after He had been robed in purple and crowned with thorns is a typical scene from the Saturnalia, at the celebration of which, during the five days of Reversal which were customary, a condemned prisoner would play the part of the Mock-

King, who was later put to death. This was a very ancient ritual which would have been well understood by the soldiers. They hailed Him King in jest.

After the scourging there is in the Fourth Gospel further conversation in the Judgment Hall where Pilate in fear, reluctant to condemn Jesus, seeks to discover who He is, and Jesus is silent.

In the Acts of Pilate there is a significant private colloquy not included in the Gospel text:

> "Then the governor commanded all Jews to go out from the Judgment Hall and he called Jesus to him: 'What shall I do with thee?' Jesus saith unto Pilate: 'Do as it hath been given thee'. Pilate saith: 'How hath it been given?' Jesus saith: 'Moses and the prophets did foretell concerning my death and rising again'."

All that remains of this interchange in the Gospel is the sentence:

> "Thou couldest have had no power against me except it were given thee from above."
>
> (*John* XIX:11)

In all the Gospels and in the Acts of Pilate, Pilate's reluctance to condemn Jesus is emphasized. In St.John the turning-point is shewn to be the cry of the Jews: "If thou let this man go, thou art not Ceasar's friend". At this point there is the final question: "Shall I crucify your King?" and the answer: "We have no king but Ceasar", whereupon Jesus is delivered to be crucified.

In St.John's account He carries His own cross. The place of the Crucifixion, Golgotha, which all knew meant "the place of a skull", has profound significance, for the skull was the symbol in the Mysteries of the *Whole Man*.

Within the brain the whole man is represented, and without the brain to register suffering there would be no suffering. Pilate's inscription was surely written from an inner prompting, so that it could shine out in letters of fire until the end of the Aeon.

The only words from the Cross that are recorded by St.John are the simple sayings: "Woman, behold thy son" (to His Mother), "Behold thy Mother" (to John), "I thirst" and "It is finished". Reference has already been made to the verses XIX:26-30, which are differently rendered in a codex of the Fourth Gospel preserved in the archives of the Templars of St.John of Jerusalem.

> "He saith to His mother: 'Weep not; I go to my Father and to Eternal Life. Behold thy Son, He will keep My place'. Then saith He to the Disciple: 'Behold, thy Mother!' Then, bowing His head, He breathed forth His Spirit."

The words: "*He will keep My place*", belonged to a secret tradition and could not be inserted in the Scriptures which were to be made available to the Church of Peter, which was to be exoteric.

It is said that Jesus, knowing that all things were now accomplished, that the scripture might be fulfilled, saith, "I thirst". In response to His cry he was given a sponge of vinegar to drink on the end of a stalk of hyssop, in accordance with the ritual in the Greek Mysteries where the candidate *drinks the cup of life to the dregs*, and the final words, "It is finished" refer to this.

Hyssop was used to mark the thresholds of the houses of the Children of Israel with blood which gave this passage significance also for the Jews. The Greek word, tetelestai, expresses a shout of victory; thus it is described in all the Synoptic Gospels.

Jesus died at the ninth hour, the hour when the sacrificial lamb was slain in the temple. He was the Lamb slain for Passover, yet the Jews in their ignorance kept the Passover after sunset.

The fulfilment of various prophecies is pointed out in St.John's account of the Crucifixion. In Exodus, XII, instructions for the Passover are given to Moses and Aaron. One of these instructions is that not a bone of the Lamb should be broken. St.John understood that as Jesus was the Passover Lamb not a bone of Him should be broken, for the institution of the Passover heralded His death. The most mysterious prophecy is that of Zechariah who foretold:

> "So they weighed for my price thirty pieces of silver. And the Lord said unto me, 'Cast it unto the potter, a goodly price that I was prized at of them'. And I took the thirty pieces of silver, and cast them to the potter in the house of the Lord."
>
> (*Zechariah* XI:12-13)

The compensation paid for a lost animal by Jewish Law was thirty pieces of silver. The prophets were clairvoyant and had the faculty of tuning in to the vibrations of cosmic events.

The most important incident of the Crucifixion by St.John is of the piercing of the side, which occurs only in this text:

> "But one of the soldiers with a spear pierced his side and forthwith came there out blood and water. And he that saw it bare record, and his record is true: and he knoweth that he saith true, that ye might believe".
>
> (*John* XIX:34-35)

The blood and water together are proof of the death of a human being. The Rev. William Barclay suggests that

Jesus had died literally of a broken heart which flooded the pericardium, so that blood and water were mingled when this was pierced by the spear of Longinus. The piercing of the side of Jesus seems to link up with the Dance of Jesus, where it is said: "I would be pierced and I would pierce". Thus the prophecy: "They shall look on him whom they have pierced" (*Zechariah* XII:10) is fulfilled. And the One who is pierced can pierce the heart of Man with a Ray of Light so that He may enter.

The blood of the Saviour had to fall on the Earth itself to symbolise the regeneration of Mankind and the planet itself. The esoteric legend of the Holy Grail, the Cup in which Joseph of Arimathea caught the blood of Christ, preserves the mystery of the secret of immortal life which the Cup contained for those who could find it and drink therefrom.

In the Acts of John the Dance of Jesus is followed by the description of St.John's vision of Christ on the Mount of Olives, where out of the Light a Voice came telling him that, although He was being crucified down below in the eyes of the multitude, in the divine part of His Being He was high above all that was happening down below and was able to tell John of the Mystery of the Cross, not the Cross of wood, but the Cross of Light which separates what is above from what is below. The divine voice also tells John of the Mystery of suffering, as it is spoken of in the Dance, and says:

> "Thou hearest that I suffered, yet did I not suffer; that I suffered not, yet did I suffer; that I was pierced, yet was not smitten; hanged, and I was not hanged; that blood flowed from me, and it flowed not; and, in a word, what they say of me, that befell me not, but what they say not, that did I suffer. Perceive thou therefore in me slaying of the Word

> (Logos), the piercing of the Word, the blood of the Word, the wound of the Word, the hanging up of the Word, the suffering of the Word, the nailing of the Word, the death of the Word. And so speak I, separating off the manhood. Perceive thou therefore in the first place the Word: then shalt thou perceive the Lord, and in the third place the man and what he hath suffered."

Here we are given a clue to the inner meaning of the Crucifixion which reveals to us the continuous suffering within Everyman of what is divine in us which is wounded day after day until the man is redeemed, Divine suffering cannot be comprehended by Man until his consciousness is raised through At-one-ment with is own divinity. St.John, in the Acts of John, concludes the narration of his vision with the following words:

> "Be ye also persuaded, therefore, beloved, that it is not a man whom I preach unto to worship, but God unchangeable, God invincible, God higher than all authority and all power, and elder and mightier than all angels and creatures that are named, and all aeons. If then ye abide in Him, and are builded up in Him, ye shall possess your soul indestructible."

APPENDIX

A NOTE ON THE RESURRECTION

THROUGHOUT the Fourth Gospel it is made clear that Jesus came into incarnation through the Will of God to fulfil a certain purpose – to reconcile Man to Himself. Responsibility for the Crucifixion was in the Will of the Father which He obeyed. Many people were used as instruments – instruments would have to expiate their guilt but the ultimate responsibility was not theirs. The later suffering of Judas and Pilate, Annas and Caiaphas, are recorded. In the Gospel of St.John we read how Jesus consciously antagonized the Jews, all of whom acted from fear when they sought his life.

The cleansing of the Temple caused financial loss to the family of the High Priest as sacrificial birds and animals without blemish had been sold there at an exorbitant price for years to the profit of Annas, the former High Priest, and Caiaphas, his son-in-law. Thus Jesus had become a danger to them in the place where they were vulnerable – their love of riches. The Jews moreover feared that if one of their number stirred up trouble they might lose their privileges. Pilate was known to be vulnerable in his position as Roman Governor as certain incidents in his past were discreditable. He could not risk further question. Those who sought Jesus' death therefore were prompted by fear.

Early in the Gospel the prophecy of Jesus as to His death and resurrection is made:

> "Then answered the Jews and said unto him, 'What sign shewest thou unto us, seeing that thou doest these things?' Jesus answered and said unto them, 'Destroy this temple,

and in three days I will raise it up'. Then said the Jews, 'Forty and six years was this temple in building, and wilt thou rear it up in three days?' But he spake of the temple of his body. When therefore he was raised from the dead, his disciples remembered that he had said this unto them; and they believed the scripture, and the word which Jesus had said."

(*John* II:18-22)

The Temple in Jerusalem, like all sacred places of worship, was a symbol of Man. It was built by divine command to remind the Jews that Man contained within the centre of himself a holy, secret place where he could be in the presence of God.

Only the priest could enter the Holy of Holies, which meant that only through that part of his being which could serve what is higher could he commune with God. Here the Ark was kept, symbol of the Ark in oneself.

The outer court was pro-fane (literally beyond the Temple), representing that part of a man which received impact of life and tended to forget the reason why he was born. The body of the Temple was used for worship according to the ritual laid down. In the time of Christ it was not a place of teaching, for this was customarily carried on in the synagogues. Jesus taught in the Temple. It is as though He wished to emphasize that He was the Temple.

In the Fourth Gospel it is recorded that He attended the Temple festivals during a period of three years and it was at these times that He gave instruction to those who spoke with Him, Pharisees, Sadducees, Scribes, as well as to His disciples. St.Matthew records that at his death "the veil of the temple was rent in twain from the top to the bottom". This was a Sign of At-one-ment, the possibility of which He had come down to reveal to men, in that when He had suffered crucifixion by those who did not accept His divinity, the Divine Light in Him was no longer veiled but could illumine the whole Temple.

Herein lies the mystery of the Resurrection. Jesus shews that He was conscious in the Glorious Body of Light, which had power to de-materialize the atoms of the physical body and assemble them again when it was expedient to convince His disciples and friends of His continuing presence and the truth of His Resurrection. This is why Jesus made Thomas touch him and shared a meal with the disciples, giving proof that it was a physical body that He inhabited and not the subtle body in which men find themselves after death if they have not attained to the Body of Light.

The possibility of attaining to this Resurrection Body was known to priests of all Great Religions. Its powers of de-materializing have been forgotten by those who teach that Man will rise again in the body which he has inhabited on earth. Many commentators have searched the Gospels in vain for evidence of those who could have moved the stone from the mouth of the sepulchre. One who had power over the atoms of the physical body would have power also over the mineral world. The Gospel Drama shews the Way to the attainment of Life Eternal in the Body of Light, called by Rodney Collin the Electronic Body. He speaks of the appearances after the Resurrection:

> "Christ was then able to project a *new* physical body, or many such bodies, in different places, *after the original body had been destroyed.* Suddenly two friends, walking in the country to Emmaus, find a physical Christ beside them: the same day another Christ appears to disciples inside a locked

room: a week later there is another appearance to Thomas under similar conditions: while a fourth Christ comes to disciples fishing, across the Lake of Tiberias. In each case, a very curious proof of physical existence is made *by the appearing Christ himself*, who insists upon eating food or being touched. This would seem curiously irrelevant, were its aim not to shew that the appearance is no hallucination, even no vision, but an actual physical body. For to those who understood, this alone would be proof that Christ had reached a realm where he could create and destroy bodies at will, that is, he had complete freedom of all vehicles, and was working in the spirit from the electronic world."

(*The Theory of Eternal Life* page 114)

Beryl Pogson (1895-1967)

Beryl Pogson was a pupil of Dr. Maurice Nicoll for nineteen years and his secretary for fourteen years and was one of the small group who lived with him and Mrs. Nicoll at the houses where The Work was carried on: Tyeponds, Birdlip, Quaremead and Great Amwell House.

Many of her writings have been published only privately for the benefit of her students and groups. Now for the first time much of her Teaching has been republished and is now more widely known.

Beryl Pogson taught that the aim of all religion is to change man's level of Being and to teach him to live according to his own divinely ordained nature. Every religion has an inner teaching which is basically the same, through which man can seek to reach his highest destiny.

This teaching is periodically renewed throughout the ages. Efforts are made to awaken man through the coming of great teachers, by the lives of holy men and women and the work of artists, writers, and musicians – many of whom have come under the influence of esoteric schools in all lands and at all periods up to the present day. Practical Work Teaching was always given.

Beryl Pogson had a sense of urgency about The Work and an inner certainty of what she should do. She always sought to form a group into a focus of reality which could be used by a higher power. We saw our task, firstly in the continuing need to work on ourselves individually, secondly through sharing with the group at meetings and in our gatherings and activities – to make life our teacher – and thirdly to relate our efforts to the work of Conscious Humanity.

During the last ten years of her life she was taking as many as six Group meetings a week, and daily meetings during sessions at The Dicker, Sussex. These were quite informal lectures followed by questions, but quite often she would ask for a question at the beginning and a discussion would take its course from the question asked. She often made connections between The Work and sacred books, literature, plays and poetry as will be seen in these books. At the meeting there were members of her group who were from different backgrounds and different stages of The Work yet with a unity of purpose. Her Work teaching was based on *The Psychological Commentaries on the Teachings of G.I. Gurdjieff and P.D. Ouspensky* by Maurice Nicoll, and of course, on Gurdjieff's and Ouspensky's own writings.

The Editor

Beryl Pogson in 1965

Beryl Pogson and Maurice Nicoll in 1949

Available from Eureka Editions:

P.D. Ouspensky *A Record of Meetings*
P.D. Ouspensky *A Further Record*
Bob Hunter ***P.D. Ouspensky: Pioneer of the Fourth Way***
Bob Hunter ***The True Myth*** Beryl Pogson's teaching on Gurdjieff's *All and Everything*
Bob Hunter ***A Pupil's Postscript***
Bob Hunter/Beryl Pogson ***Brighton Work Talks***
Maurice Nicoll ***Psychological Commentaries on the Teaching of Gurdjieff & Ouspensky*** 6 Vols.
Maurice Nicoll ***The New Man***
Maurice Nicoll ***The Mark***
Maurice Nicoll ***Living Time***
Maurice Nicoll ***Selections from Meetings in 1953***
Maurice Nicoll ***Simple Explanation of Work Ideas***
Maurice Nicoll ***Notes taken at meetings in 1934***
A Few Recollections of Dr Nicoll and Amwell 1949-1953
Beryl Pogson ***Royalty of Nature***
Beryl Pogson ***In the East My Pleasure Lies***
Beryl Pogson ***Meeting taken by Beryl Pogson***
Beryl Pogson ***Maurice Nicoll: A Portrait***
Beryl Pogson ***Commentary on the Fourth Gospel***
Beryl Pogson/Bob Hunter ***Mind and Energy***
Bob Hunter ***Catherine Nicoll - A Wakeful Wife***
Beryl Pogson & Others ***Unforgotten Fragments***
Beryl Pogson & Others ***Centenary Fragments***
Beryl Pogson ***Work Talks at The Dicker***
Beryl Pogson ***More Work Talks***
Bob Hunter ***Ronald Oldham: A Life in three Acts***
Ronald & Muriel Oldham ***Work Teachings - Work Poems***
Samuel Copley ***Portrait of a Vertical Man: Maurice Nicoll***
Anon. ***Words on the Work***
Anon. ***A Recapitulation of the Lord's prayer***
Anon. ***A Point in the Work*** (Two Volumes)
Irmis Popoff ***Gurdjieff*** His Work-On Myself-With Others-For the Work
Solange Claustres ***G.I.Gurdjieff***
Paul Beekman Taylor ***The Philosophy of G.I.Gurdjieff***
Paul Beekman Taylor ***Gurdjieff's Invention of America***
Paul Beekman Taylor ***G.I.Gurdjieff: A New Life***
Paul Beekman Taylor ***Gurdjieff in the Public Eye***

Eureka Editions
info@eurekaeditions.com
www.eurekaeditions.com

THIS EDITION PUBLISHED
E-BOOK
IN MARCH 2020

AND PRINTED ON DEMAND
BY AMAZON

HERENSTRAAT 4 A
3512 KC UTRECHT - THE NETHERLANDS

www.eurekaeditions.com
info@eurekaeditions.com

Printed in Great Britain
by Amazon

62595553R00050